D1348572

AIRPLANES

by Jenny Fretland VanVoorst

pogo

Ideas for Parents and Teachers

Pogo Books let children practice reading informational text while introducing them to nonfiction features such as headings, labels, sidebars, maps, and diagrams, as well as a table of contents, glossary, and index.

Carefully leveled text with a strong photo match offers early fluent readers the support they need to succeed.

Before Reading

• "Walk" through the book and point out the various nonfiction features. Ask the student what purpose each feature serves.

• Look at the glossary together. Read and discuss the words.

Read the Book

• Have the child read the book independently.

• Invite him or her to list questions that arise from reading.

After Reading

• Discuss the child's questions. Talk about how he or she might find answers to those questions.

• Prompt the child to think more. Ask: Have you ever flown on an airplane before? Does learning how airplanes work make the experience seem safer?

Pogo Books are published by Jump!
5357 Penn Avenue South
Minneapolis, MN 55419
www.jumplibrary.com

Copyright © 2018 Jump!
International copyright reserved in all countries.
No part of this book may be reproduced in any form without written permission from the publisher.

Library of Congress Cataloging-in-Publication Data

Names: Fretland VanVoorst, Jenny, 1972- author.
Title: Airplanes / by Jenny Fretland VanVoorst.
Description: Minneapolis, MN : Jump!, Inc., [2018]
Series: How does it work? | Audience: Ages 7-10.
"Pogo Books are published by Jump!"
Includes bibliographical references and index.
Identifiers: LCCN 2017040252 (print)
LCCN 2017045310 (ebook) | ISBN 9781624966941 (ebook) | ISBN 9781620319000 (hardcover : alk. paper)
ISBN 9781620319017 (pbk.)
Subjects: LCSH: Airplanes–Juvenile literature.
Classification: LCC TL547 (ebook) | LCC TL547 .F757 2018 (print) | DDC 629.133/34—dc23
LC record available at https://lccn.loc.gov/2017040252

Editor: Jenna Trnka
Book Designer: Leah Sanders
Photo Researcher: Leah Sanders

Photo Credits: Vibrant Image Studio/Shutterstock, cover; Rebius/Shutterstock, 1; David Acosta Allely/Shutterstock, 3; TinnaPong/Shutterstock, 4; Kletr/Shutterstock, 5; Alexey Y. Petrov/Shutterstock, 6-7; Jag_cz/Shutterstock, 8-9; Carlos E. Santa Maria/Shutterstock, 10-11; Andrey Khachatryan/Shutterstock, 12; razorbeam/Shutterstock, 13; dell640/iStock, 14-15; bkindler/iStock, 16; Aureliy/Shutterstock, 17; sumroeng chinnapan/Shutterstock, 18-19 (background); Zhou Eka/Shutterstock, 18-19 (plane); SerrNovik/iStock, 20-21; Sergey Novikov/Shutterstock, 23.

Printed in the United States of America at Corporate Graphics in North Mankato, Minnesota.

TABLE OF CONTENTS

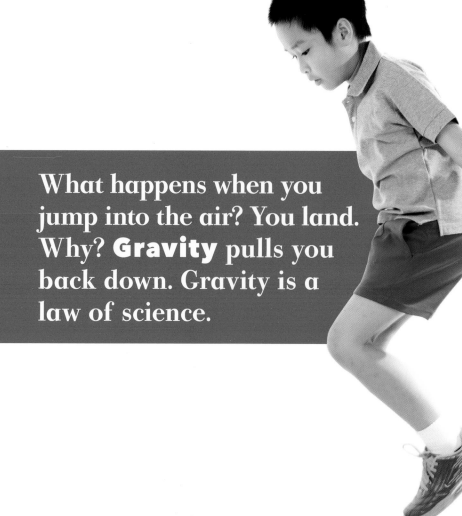

CHAPTER 1

ENGINES

What happens when you jump into the air? You land. Why? **Gravity** pulls you back down. Gravity is a law of science.

But an airplane can fly high in the sky for hours. How do airplanes work? Let's find out!

Airplanes work by balancing **physics** forces. Four forces affect a plane. They are **thrust**, **drag**, **lift**, and gravity. An airplane is designed to keep these forces in balance.

gravity

thrust

drag

lift

thrust

engine

exhaust

Thrust is the force that moves the plane forward. The engines help with this. Jet engines burn fuel. **Exhaust** is pushed out the back. The power of this backward force pushes the plane forward.

DID YOU KNOW?

Thrust is balanced by another force. It is drag. This **resistance** is caused by tiny air particles. They slow the plane down.

A plane has many parts. They work together to make it take off, fly, and land. These include engines, fuel tanks, wheels, and **radar**.

DID YOU KNOW?

Big planes can hold about 25,000 times as much fuel as a car. They have multiple fuel tanks.

radar

CHAPTER 2

· ·

WINGS

A plane's engines push it forward. Its movement causes air to flow over the wings.

The wings on a plane have a special shape. They have a curved top and a flat bottom. This shape maximizes lift.

The shape changes the air pressure around the wings. How? The moving air is forced downward. The downward-moving air pushes the plane up. This upward force is called lift. It works against gravity. It keeps the plane in the air.

gravity

lift

CHAPTER 3
CONTROLS

A plane's engines move it forward. Its wings move it upward. But how is it controlled once it is up and moving?

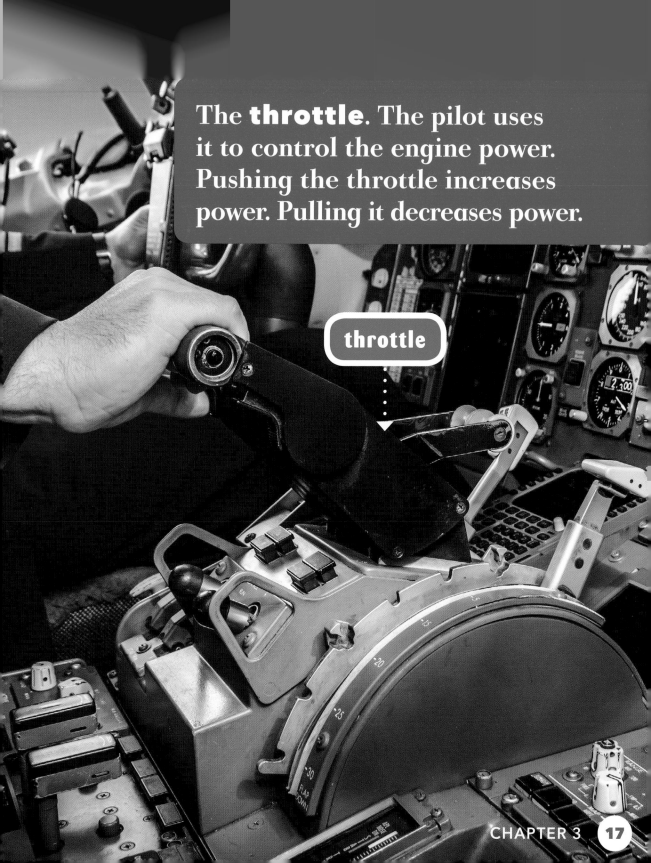

The **throttle**. The pilot uses it to control the engine power. Pushing the throttle increases power. Pulling it decreases power.

throttle

Steering is different. The air must flow differently over each wing. The pilot controls flaps on the wings. The flaps move the plane up and down. They move it side to side.

TAKE A LOOK!

Here are some of the parts that help control a plane:

RUDDER
The rudder controls the motion of a plane from side to side. Together, the rudder and the ailerons turn the plane.

ELEVATORS
These control the **pitch** of the plane. Lowering them makes the plane go down. Raising them makes the plane go up.

AILERONS
These flaps on the wings raise and lower. The pilot moves them to control the plane.

So what makes airplanes fly? Equipment that puts physics to work.

Airplanes seem to work like magic. But they are science all the way!

ACTIVITIES & TOOLS

TRY THIS!

PAPER AIRPLANE STEERING

How can you steer a paper plane while in flight? The trick is to get one wing to create more lift than the other.

What You Need:
- paper
- scissors
- paper clip

1. First, make a paper plane. Toss it a few times to make sure it flies straight. Adjust your folds or your design as necessary.

2. Next, cut the backs of the wings to make some ailerons. Tilt them up and down, and then try some test flights. What effect do they have in different positions?

3. Now try tilting one up and one down. What difference does that make?

4. Now add a paper clip to one wing to make that side heavier. What happens?

5. Then try making a new plane with one wing bigger than the other. What is the result?

6. What have you learned about how changes to the plane's wings control steering?

GLOSSARY

drag: The force acting on an airplane to slow it down as it moves through the air.

exhaust: The gas that escapes from an engine.

gravity: The attraction of the earth for bodies at or near its surface.

lift: An upward force that opposes the pull of gravity.

physics: The science that deals with matter and energy and their actions upon each other in the fields of mechanics, heat, light, electricity, sound, and the atomic nucleus.

pitch: Movement or position up and down.

radar: A device that uses radio waves to find out information, such as an object's position and speed.

resistance: An opposing or slowing force.

throttle: An instrument that controls the flow of fuel to an engine.

thrust: The force, created by engines, that drives an airplane forward.

INDEX

TO LEARN MORE

Learning more is as easy as 1, 2, 3.

1) Go to www.factsurfer.com

2) Enter "airplanes" into the search box.

3) Click the "Surf" button to see a list of websites.

With factsurfer, finding more information is just a click away.